Sound Waves and Communication

Jenna Winterberg

Consultant

Michelle Alfonsi
Engineer, Southern California
Aerospace Industry

Publishing Credits

Rachelle Cracchiolo, M.S.Ed., *Publisher*
Conni Medina, M.A.Ed., *Managing Editor*
Diana Kenney, M.A.Ed., NBCT, *Senior Editor*
Dona Herweck Rice, *Series Developer*
Robin Erickson, *Multimedia Designer*
Timothy Bradley, *Illustrator*

Image Credits: Cover, p.1 Shutterstock; p.12 AF archive / Alamy; p.22 A. T. Willett / Alamy; p.18 Grace Alba; pp.4, 10, 11, 12, 15, 16, 22, 23, 26, 27 iStock; p.7 Library of Congress (LC-DIG-ppprs-00369); pp.28, 29 Janelle Bell-Martin; p.26 Jim Varney / Science Photo Library; p.19 NASA; p.17 NOAA; p.16 Phillipe Saada / Science Source; p.11 Ted Kinsman / Science Source; all other images from Shutterstock.

Web links and URL addresses included in this book are public domain and may be subject to changes or alterations of content after publication by Teacher Created Materials. Teacher Created Materials does not take responsibility for the accuracy or future relevance and appropriateness of any web links or URL addresses included in this book after publication. Please contact us if you come across any inappropriate or inaccurate web links and URL addresses and we will correct them in future printings.

Library of Congress Cataloging-in-Publication Data

Winterberg, Jenna, author.
  Sound waves and communication / Jenna Winterberg.
     pages cm
     Summary: "Beep, beep, beep! Whirrrr. From loud and annoying to peaceful and relaxing, sounds are an ever-present part of life. Sound not only helps us send messages to one another, but also tells us about our world."-- Provided by publisher.
     Audience: Grades 4 to 6.
     Includes index.
     ISBN 978-1-4807-4684-8 (pbk.)
  1. Sound--Juvenile literature. 2. Sound-waves--Juvenile literature. I. Title.
     QC225.5.W56 2016
     534--dc23
                          2014045207

Teacher Created Materials

5301 Oceanus Drive
Huntington Beach, CA 92649-1030
http://www.tcmpub.com
ISBN 978-1-4807-4684-8

Table of Contents

Power of Sound

Sound helps us to communicate. We use it to chat with our parents. We depend on it when we call a friend. It's an important part of watching our "can't miss" shows on TV. And it's the most important thing when we put on our headphones.

Humans aren't the only ones using sound. The animal kingdom is alive with noise. From chirping and buzzing to mewing and howling, bugs, birds, and critters use sound to share information and even to find their way.

Sometimes, sound prevents communication. It's hard to hear someone else talk over loud music. And the roar of a crowd can make it hard for football players to hear a quarterback's calls. Construction, airplanes, and trucks all make enough noise to drown out other sounds, too.

Good or bad, sound surrounds us. Science can tell us a lot about sounds soft and loud, pleasing and annoying. It even allows us to detect and measure sounds we can't hear.

Waves of Sound

Sound is a type of energy that travels in waves. The word *wave* typically brings to mind ocean waves and surfers that ride them, or the way a rope curls up and down with a flick of a wrist. These kinds of up-and-down wave patterns are made up of **transverse waves**. Transverse waves, like light waves, travel in only one direction. Sound waves work differently.

Sound waves act more like the ripples you might see in a pond when skipping stones. Instead of traveling up and down in one direction, sound waves move out in all directions. This type of wave is referred to as a **longitudinal** (lon-ji-TOOD-n-l) **wave**. A ripple starts out strong but then gradually disappears. In the same way, sound waves are strongest at the point at which they started. They lose energy the farther they get from the source. Then, they too, disappear.

Sound waves can travel through water like ripples. They also travel through solids. But most often, we experience sound as it travels through the air.

Acousticophobia (uh-KOO-stik-oh-FOH-bee-uh) is the fear of sound or noise.

Space Observers?

While sound waves can't travel through space, radio waves can. It takes time for the waves to travel through space. If any space aliens were to pick up on our radio waves, they would end up watching old TV shows. Way out at the star Regalus, they would be watching the first-ever baseball game on TV!

7

Clap your hands. The action creates a vibration in the air, which pushes **particles** of air together. When air **molecules** are pressed together, the air becomes **compressed**. A pressure wave is created.

That area where the air is under high pressure makes up the **crest**, or peak, of the sound wave. The molecules that moved into that area had to come from somewhere. They moved into that space from the air nearby. As a result, a pocket forms next to the high-pressure area where the molecules are more spread out. This area of low pressure is the sound wave's **trough**.

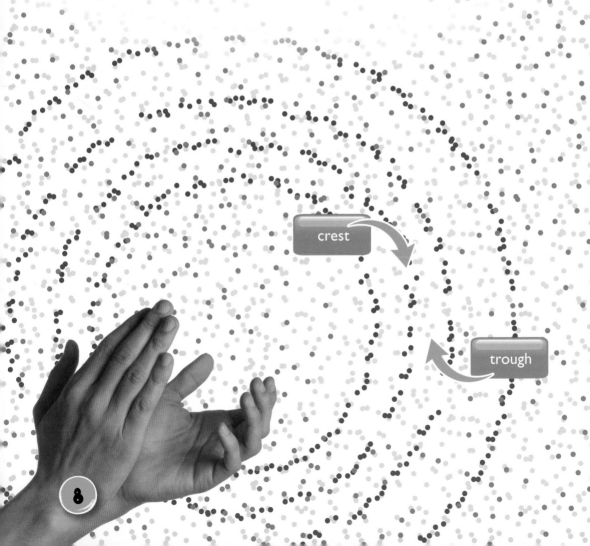

crest

trough

Echoes All Around

When sound waves strike a hard, smooth surface, they bounce off. This creates an echo. Most of the sounds we hear are really a combination of the original sound and the echo from walls, floors, and other surfaces nearby.

This high-and-low wave pattern continues. As it ripples out, it pushes the vibration of your clap forward. The molecules don't travel. But the sound travels because the vibrating molecules bump into one another. This causes a chain reaction, pushing the wave on. The wave carries the sound away from the source. In time, it will lose energy and flatten.

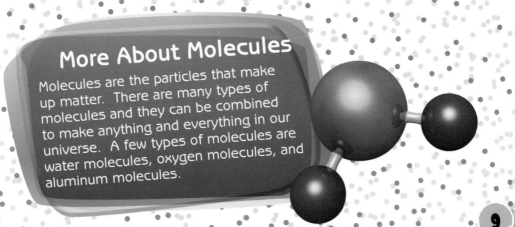

More About Molecules

Molecules are the particles that make up matter. There are many types of molecules and they can be combined to make anything and everything in our universe. A few types of molecules are water molecules, oxygen molecules, and aluminum molecules.

Measuring Sound

We don't often see or feel sound. We hear it. The human ear responds to changes in pressure waves. And it senses that as sound.

When you clapped your hands, was the sound loud? Could you clap more loudly?

The loudness, or **volume**, of a sound results from how tightly the molecules are pressed together. The more energy a vibration has, the tighter the particles and the louder the sound.

When you turn up the volume on your TV, you increase the energy of the vibration. Your action packs the molecules more tightly. That makes the sound louder.

Sound vs. Light

Unlike light waves, sound waves always travel through something. Sometimes that is something that you can see or feel, such as a wall or a speaker. Most of the time, sound travels through the air. That is why we can't hear sound in space—there is no air in space.

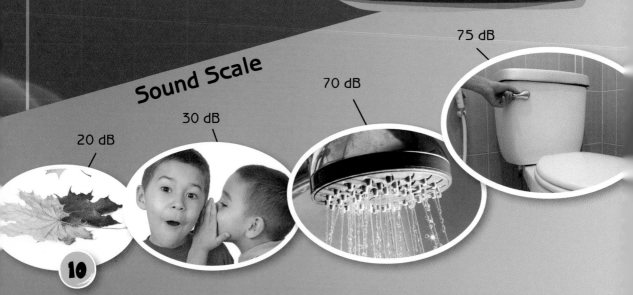

Sound Scale

20 dB

30 dB

70 dB

75 dB

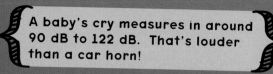
We measure a sound's volume in **decibels** (dB). This is a measure of intensity that tells us how much energy a sound wave has. The quietest sounds we can hear are about 10 dB, the sound of normal breathing. Sounds of 130 dB can be painful; a jet plane takes off at about 140 dB. A whisper has a low intensity, measuring about 30 dB. When people talk, that sound is 40 dB. Talking is only 10 dB louder than whispering. But each 10 dB of sound multiplies intensity by 10, so talking is 100 times more intense.

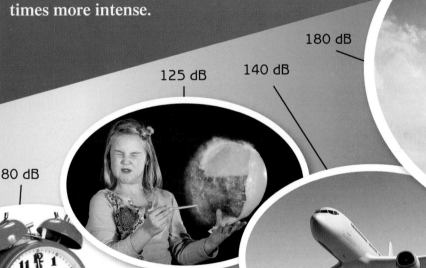

80 dB

125 dB

140 dB

180 dB

Danger Zone

Constant sound can cause headaches and illness, even if it's not loud. But high-decibel sounds are far more damaging. In a short time, 120 dB sounds can cause hearing loss. Any noise above 130 dB will cause the listener pain.

The amount of energy isn't the only thing we measure when it comes to sound. We also look at **wavelength**. That's the distance between the two peaks of the same wave.

Waves can be short and close together. They also can be long and spread apart. When waves are short, sound has a high **frequency**. Frequency refers to how many times a particle vibrates in a second. A high frequency comes with a high **pitch**. A whistle has a high pitch, so we know it also has a high frequency.

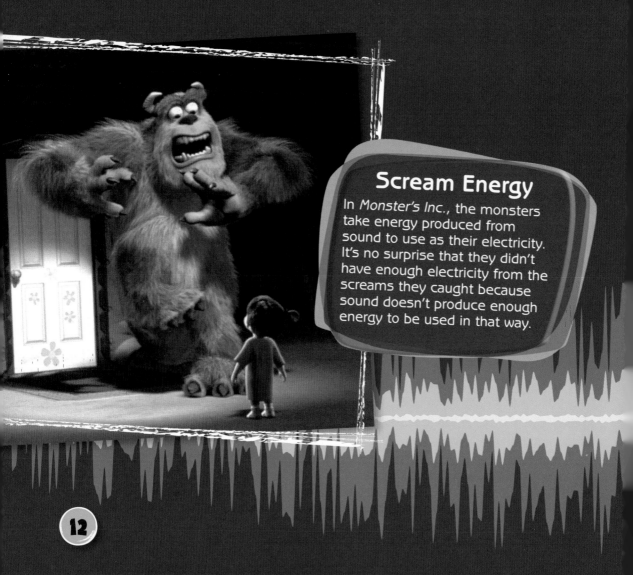

Scream Energy

In *Monster's Inc.*, the monsters take energy produced from sound to use as their electricity. It's no surprise that they didn't have enough electricity from the screams they caught because sound doesn't produce enough energy to be used in that way.

Short wavelengths create high frequencies. They sound shrill in pitch, like a mouse's squeak. Long wavelengths produce low frequencies. They sound deep in pitch, like a lion's roar. Frequency is measured in hertz (Hz). Humans can detect sounds between 20 Hz and 20,000 Hz.

The intensity of a sound can vary with distance. Decibels decrease when we are farther from the sound's source because the wave loses energy. But frequency and pitch remain constant. The wavelength of a sound doesn't alter even when the wave loses energy.

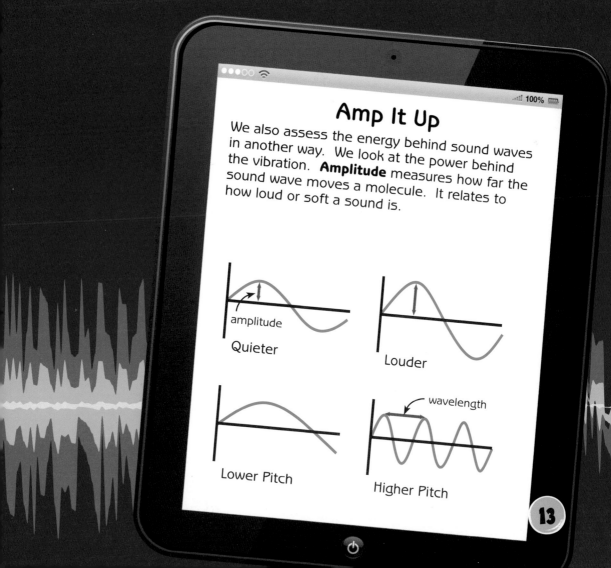

Amp It Up

We also assess the energy behind sound waves in another way. We look at the power behind the vibration. **Amplitude** measures how far the sound wave moves a molecule. It relates to how loud or soft a sound is.

amplitude

Quieter

Louder

Lower Pitch

wavelength

Higher Pitch

There are times when it seems like the pitch of a sound rises and falls. This occurs when the sound's source is in motion. Watch an auto race on TV and listen as the cars pass by. The vroom of the engine becomes a *veeeeeeerrrrooooom*. It starts at a higher pitch when it's approaching. When it's in front of the viewer, the pitch is true to life. And then, as the vehicle leaves, the pitch seems to drop lower.

Emergency vehicles produce a similar effect. When their sirens approach, the sound seems very shrill. But after they pass, the pitch seems to grow deeper. This an example of the **Doppler effect** at work.

When a sound's source is moving, it sends out a sound wave and then travels a short way before the next wave. So, the waves in front of the source become pressed together, and the waves behind become stretched apart. This makes the wavelengths in front of the source shorter and the pitch higher. The wavelength behind the source is longer, and the pitch is lower.

Next time you play Marco Polo in the pool, use decibel changes and the Doppler effect to your advantage to locate your friends!

Jumping Rice

Stretch plastic wrap across the top of a bowl and spread rice on top. Hold a cookie tray over the center of the bowl. Bang the tray with a wooden spoon and watch what happens to the rice. What might happen if the bowl and the tray were touching? What do you think the Doppler effect would do?

The Doppler Effect

Dogs can hear whistles we cannot. And cats hear the high frequency calls of the bugs, birds, and mice they hunt! The world is full of sounds that are too high-pitched for us to hear. These noises above 20,000 Hz are called *ultrasonic*. Animals use sounds in this range to communicate. Sometimes, they even use them to navigate. Grasshoppers use this high range to seek out mates. And bats have poor sight, so they use **ultrasounds** to find their way. Dolphins use ultrasound for both purposes!

Just because humans can't hear it doesn't mean we can't use it! These sound beams can create heat when they vibrate. That allows them to etch, drill, and even weld. High-power ultrasound can be used instead of surgery. It's used to break up kidney stones still inside the body. Low-power ultrasound works like sonar. It echoes from inside the body. That echo creates a wavy image, allowing us to see organs, muscle, and tissue. We use ultrasound to scan the heart to look for problems. We also check on babies before they're born thanks to this technology.

Doppler ultrasound of an unborn baby

16

Sounding Out Location

Ships use sonar to map the seafloor. Sonar sends pulses of sound waves into the water. Echoes return to indicate where surfaces are. It's navigation by echo. In nature, animals like bats and dolphins use echolocation (ek-oh-loh-KEY-shuhn) the same way.

Just as some sounds are too high for us to hear, a number of sounds are too low for us to hear. Any sound below 20 Hz is called an **infrasound**.

Many animals use infrasound. Whales call out to each other at very low frequencies. They "sing" to attract mates in the same way. Some species use these low sounds to stun prey! Elephants, rhinos, and even tigers communicate with infrasound.

Whale Songs

Each species of whale uses a different sound to communicate. Sounds are grouped by species and location. There's such a variety of sounds that researchers are asking for your help in understanding what whales are saying! You can go online to **http://whale.fm** to help scientists match whale sounds.

Notes from the Sun

Scientists measured the vibrations of the sun's surface. They translated these vibrations into sound waves with a computer. The sun pulses with complex vibrations. Additional waves both bounce off the surface of the sun and travel to its core, making it ring like cathedral bells—with different notes, volume, and pitches.

We humans collect data on infrasound. We use it to find resources buried deep in the earth. We also use it to predict volcanic eruptions and other natural events. Humans can't hear infrasound. Yet we still often sense these sound waves. Some scientists have found that these sounds can cause changes in blood pressure, breathing, and balance. They are also found to make people feel annoyed or sad.

Regular levels of infrasound can knock down objects and rattle glass and windows. Just think about what happens when a jet passes by close overhead. A strong blast of infrasound could leave vast amounts of damage in its wake.

Sound Travels

We've covered noises dolphins and whales make. So clearly, we know sound travels in water, not just in air. Sound can travel through gases, liquids, and solids. One of these must be present. But in a vacuum, as in outer space, where there are no particles for sound to move through—it's silent.

If you've ever ducked your head below water, you know sound isn't the same there. The pitch doesn't change, but the intensity of sound alters.

In liquid, molecules pack in more closely than in air. That means they bump into each other more often and more quickly. As a result, sounds travel farther and faster in water. In fact, a sound wave travels four times faster in water than in air!

The energy spreads out rapidly. And that makes sounds much less intense. That's because instead of being concentrated, the energy is sent out over a wider area.

Secret Knocks

Scuba divers can't use their voices underwater. They use hand signals, but they also send sound signals. These tap codes are patterns of sound made by knocking on their tanks.

For the same reason, more energy is needed for a sound to be heard at all. Without intensity at the source, there won't be enough energy to carry the sound.

In solids, molecules are packed even more tightly. That's why we hear only very intense sounds from behind closed doors.

Speed of Sound

Sound waves travel more or less quickly depending on what they're traveling through.

19,685 feet per second
(6,000 meters per second)

16,820 ft. per second
(5,127 m per second)

12,620 ft. per second
(3,847 m per second)

4,794 ft. per second
(1,462 m per second)

1,129 ft. per second (344 m per second)

Air Water Wood Iron Stone

The rate at which sound travels differs in air, water, and solids. But usually we're talking about air when we refer to the speed of sound.

Even in air, temperature and other factors can affect sound's speed. So, there's no set value for the speed of sound. We can do some fancy math to work it out for any situation. But on average, the speed of sound is somewhere in the 900 to 1,200 kilometers per hour (560 to 746 miles per hour) range. The average plane travels at about 800 kmh (500 mph).

There are few objects that travel faster than sound. But jets and rockets both can outpace sound waves. When an aircraft travels at the speed of sound, the speed is called *Mach 1*. When it travels faster, the flight is **supersonic**.

We know when supersonic flight occurs because of the sound barrier. As a jet or rocket nears the speed of sound, air pressure increases ahead of it. That pressure forms a barrier. For an aircraft to break through, it must travel faster than sound. This causes a shockwave and a loud blast of sound known as a *sonic boom*.

Most vehicles, such as cars and buses, have a Mach speed of less than 1. They are subsonic.

Some planes travel at Mach 1. They are transonic.

Breaking the Speed of Sound

You can have various types of objects on the Mach scale. The different speeds are called *subsonic, transonic, supersonic,* and *hypersonic.*

jet breaking the sound barrier

Jets can travel at a speed greater than Mach 1. They are supersonic.

Rockets can travel at speeds greater than Mach 5. They are hypersonic.

Sound travels only so far in nature. But we've created methods to carry it farther. We blast sounds out into crowds and even carry them with us on our phones.

To do these things, we first have to convert sound waves into electrical signals.

The microphone is a tool made to copy sound waves. It acts just like an eardrum, "hearing" vibrations. But it doesn't just listen to sound; it replicates it. A magnet within the microphone vibrates along with the sound. This causes a pulse of electricity to travel down a thin coil of wire. Each pulse is a copy of the sound wave. These copies are sent out as electrical signals.

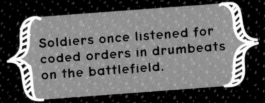

Soldiers once listened for coded orders in drumbeats on the battlefield.

Musical Vibrations

When you hold down a guitar string, the frequency of the sound wave changes. Even the thickness of the string changes the sound that is produced.

Sometimes, the signals are boosted in power by an amplifier. Then, they're sent out through speakers so that a large audience can hear the sounds. Other times, signals are stored for us to play back later. MP3s bring a whole new meaning to traveling sound!

We've even created electric instruments. These guitars, keyboards, and drums make very little sound. Instead, they make electrical signals. These can be fed directly into

Sound Ideas

From electrical signals to quiet whispers, humans use sound in numerous ways. There are sounds we hear, sounds we sense, and sounds we detect with technology.

Sound can please and soothe us, as music does. It can send a shrill warning, the way a siren might. It can also annoy us, like loud noises sometimes do.

We use sounds to communicate through speech and music. We also use sound to locate things through sonar and Doppler. We even send coded messages with sound, using drums, knocks, and taps.

Animals also use sound. It's how they find their way. Sometimes, it's how they hunt. They even use sound to attract mates.

However different these sounds and their purposes may be, they all have something in common. They are all used to communicate in some way. You just have to listen carefully for the message.

A doctor uses ultrasound to examine a patient's eye.

Decoding the ultrasonic chatter of dolphins could reveal clues to what our ocean's depths hold.

Listening to infrasonic sounds underground could help us predict earthquakes.

Think Like a Scientist

What type of surface best reflects sound waves? Experiment and find out!

What to Get

- an object that makes constant noise, such as a ticking clock or a radio

- objects of different materials and thicknesses, such as a glass plate, a plastic plate, foil wrap, and plastic wrap

- two long cardboard tubes

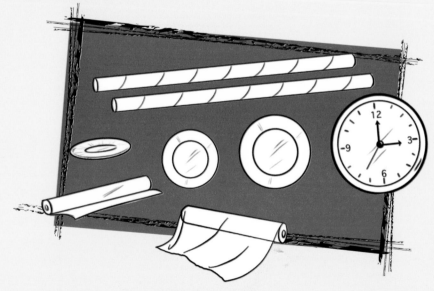

What to Do

1 Place the tubes on a table so that two ends meet at one end and are spread apart at the other.

2 Have a friend or a classmate stand where the two ends meet, covering the openings with one object at a time.

3 Where the ends are farther apart, place your noise-making object next to the opening of one tube.

4 Place your ear to the remaining opening. For each object, listen as the sound waves travel down the first tube, bounce off the object, and travel down the second tube to you.

5 Record what you hear. Is there a difference between plastic wrap and a plastic plate? Which object echoed best? Which muffled the sound most?

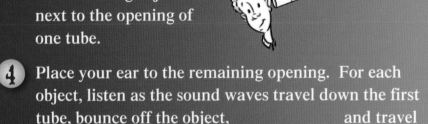

Object	Strength of Sound				
pillow	1	2	3	4	5
glass	1	2	3	4	5
foil	1	2	3	4	5
plastic	1	2	3	4	5
ceramic	1	2	3	4	5
paper	1	2	3	4	5
wood	1	2	3	4	5

Glossary

amplitude—measurement that indicates the movement or vibration of a wave

compressed—pressed together

crest—the top of a wave

decibels—units for measuring how loud a sound is

Doppler effect—an apparent shift in the frequency of sound or light due to relative motion between the source of the sound or light and the observer

frequency—number of crests or troughs of a wave that pass a given point in a specified period of time

infrasound—sound waves with a lower frequency than human hearing can detect

longitudinal wave—wave whose energy travels parallel to its direction of motion

molecules—the smallest-possible amounts of a particular substance that have all the characteristics of the substance

particles—very small pieces of a large object

pitch—the highness or lowness of a sound

supersonic—of, being, or relating to speeds from one to five times the speed of sound in air

transverse waves—waves that move back and forth perpendicular to the direction in which the waves travel

trough—the lowest point between waves

ultrasounds—sounds with higher frequencies than human hearing can detect

volume—loudness of a sound, resulting from how tightly particles are compressed

wavelength—the distance between two peaks of the same wave

Index

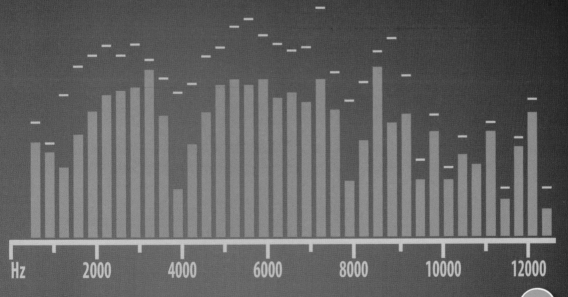

The Emotion of Sound

Can you tell a sad sound from a happy one? Spend a day listening to the voices of family and friends. How do they sound when they're upset? How do they sound when they're happy? When you listen to calming music, does it sound the same as music meant to get you dancing? What does the music on TV and in movies communicate to you? Think about what gives a sound its emotion. Is there a change in volume, amplitude, or pitch?